RORY
WITH
NO ROAR

BY MILLY HESTER

In a bright and busy forest,
where dinos stomped and soared,
there lived a dino named Rory
who couldn't make a roar.

3

He opened up his mouth so wide,
he tried with all his might!
But not a growl, not even a squeak
came out by day or night.

5

"Why don't you roar like us?"
asked Tilly with a frown.
Max said ""maybe he's too scared!"
then laughed and stomped around.

7

Rory felt so left out.
He thought he wasn't quite right.
He tried and tried and tried again,
but no roar came that night.

9

One day he saw some flying friends,
the Pterodactyls up above.
They weren't roaring, but still talked...
with flaps and signs and love!

11

So Rory flapped and waved his arms,
he tried to learn their way.
He practiced every morning,
and every single day.

13

Next time he saw his dino friends,
he didn't try to roar.
He waved and twirled and tapped his chest,
they'd never seen that before!

15

"He said it's such a lovely day!"
Said Tilly with a grin.
"And he's happy that we're here!"
Max cheered and clapped for him.

17

Soon after dinos came from far and near,
to learn from clever young Rory.
He showed them signs for love and play,
and shared his quiet story.

19

They signed "Hello!" and "How are you?"
They signed "Let's play some more!"
They found that hands and hearts could speak much louder than a roar.

21

Now no one teases Rory.
They cheer and sign and play!
His voice is made of movement,
and love he shows each day.

23

So if you cannot roar like them,
don't worry you can learn like Rory's friends,
your voice can come in many ways
And kindness never ends.

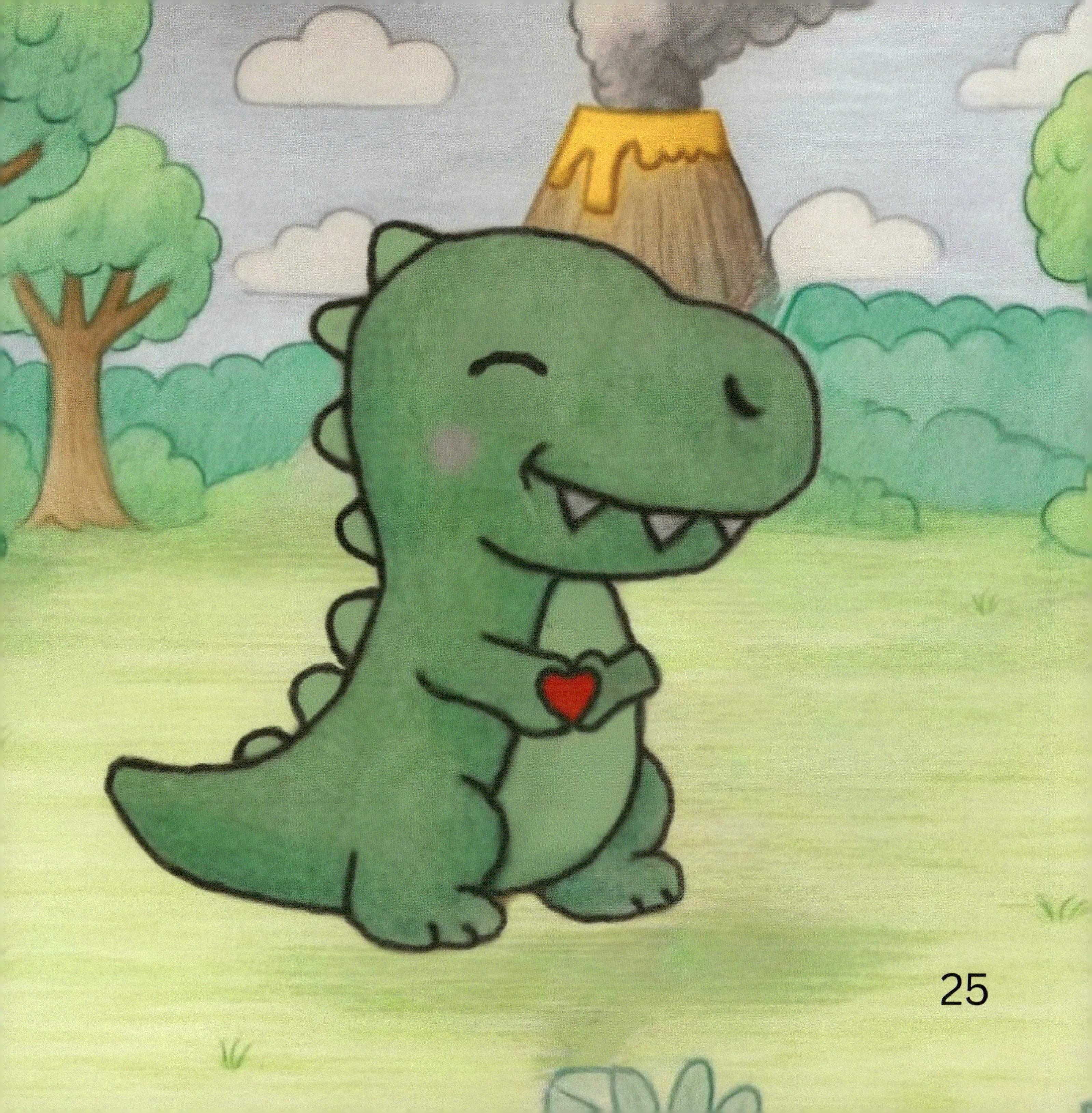

Printed in Dunstable, United Kingdom